CW01034216

PIZZA COOKBOOK

Many delicious and tasty recipes to become the best
"Pizzaiolo"

Giovanni Attanasio

Classic Crust

If you use all-purpose flour instead of bread flour for this crust, you'll end up with a denser, flatter end product. Bread flour contains more gluten and is more elastic when kneaded.

Makes crust for four 12-inch pizzas

Ingredients
2 packages active dry yeast
1½ cups warm water, about 100°F
1 teaspoon sugar
1½ teaspoons salt
6½ cups bread flour
2 tablespoons olive oil

1. In a large measuring cup, dissolve yeast in water. Let stand 5 minutes or until bubbly. Combine sugar, salt, and bread flour in the bowl of a mixer with a dough hook. Or, to mix by hand, place in a large bowl. Make a well in the flour mixture and pour in the water, followed by 1 tablespoon of oil.

2. Turn the mixer on low to blend, or begin stirring the flour into the liquid with a wooden spoon, a little at a time. When ingredients are well combined, turn the mixer on medium-low to knead for 5 minutes. If working dough by hand, turn the dough onto a well-floured work surface. Use a pressing motion with the

heels of your hands. Work dough until the mixture is slightly shiny and not too sticky to the touch.

3. The kneaded dough should be divided into four equal pieces. Store any dough not being used in a resealable bag in the refrigerator. Oil remaining dough and place in a bowl, covered, to rise for 1 hour. Punch the dough down, shape into 2 disks, and let rest for 30 minutes.

4. Grab dough by the edges, turning the disk a few inches at a time, allowing gravity to stretch the dough without tearing. Roll the dough into a crust shape or press into a pizza pan. Top as directed in recipe.

Dough for Tomorrow
Pizza dough will rise, albeit slowly, in the refrigerator. To use dough that's been refrigerated overnight, place in a covered bowl on the counter. Punch dough down, then let stand until dough reaches room temperature. Use as directed.

Pan Pizza Crust

With this recipe, you can recreate the Chicago-style deep dish pizza in your own kitchen (no matter where you live!).

Makes crust for four 12-inch pizzas

Ingredients
2 cups reduced-fat milk

2 packages active dry yeast

6 cups all-purpose flour

4 tablespoons sugar

1 teaspoon salt

5 tablespoons olive oil

1. Warm milk in the microwave to about 100°F, or just warm, not hot, to the touch.

2. In the bowl of a mixer with a dough hook, combine yeast, flour, sugar, and salt. Stir to combine. With dough hook running on low speed, slowly add the warm milk followed by 4 tablespoons olive oil.

3. Turn mixer to medium-low or proper speed for kneading. Allow mixer to knead the dough for 5 minutes or until mixture is slightly glossy and springy to the touch. If the dough seems too wet, add a small amount of flour and knead a little longer.

4. Remove dough to a lightly floured work surface. A pastry board or silicone baking sheet is good. Waxed paper or nonstick foil on the counter will do. Divide the pizza dough in half and shape into two even balls. Grease two metal or glass bowls with the remaining olive oil and place the dough balls in the bowls, turning to lightly oil the dough.

5. Cover the bowls with plastic wrap and place in a warm spot. Allow dough to rise 30 minutes or until doubled in size. Punch down. If making two pizzas, place one dough ball in a resealable plastic bag, press out the air, and refrigerate for later use. Take remaining ball and divide in half. Lightly pat each half into a flattened circle, cover, and let stand 20 to 30 minutes before placing in plans. Refrigerated dough should be allowed to come to room temperature before using.

California Thin Crust

To develop the characteristic crispness pizza lovers enjoy you need to use high-protein flour for this crust — or anything that contains 12 to 14 percent gluten (the higher the percentage the better).

Makes crust for four 12-inch pizzas

Ingredients
1 packet active dry yeast

1 cup warm water, about 100°F

2 tablespoons vegetable oil

2 teaspoons sugar

6½ cups high-protein flour

1½ teaspoons salt

1. In a large mixer bowl, combine water, yeast, oil, and sugar. Using a mixer with a dough hook, stir on low speed until the yeast dissolves and the mixture is well combined. Slowly add flour and salt. Continue stirring until a stiff ball of dough forms.

2. Place dough in a large (2-gallon) resealable plastic bag or place in a bowl and cover with plastic wrap. Refrigerate the dough for 24 hours. Remove from refrigerator and allow to come to room temperature.

3. Turn pizza onto a well-floured surface. Divide into four sections. (Return any sections that aren't being

7

used to the refrigerator.) Roll sections into very thin circles, dusting liberally with flour as you go. Prick pizza crust several times with a fork and top according to recipe directions.

Making Your Crust Super-Thin

To get your pizza super-thin, use the above recipe and a pasta roller. Run strips of dough through the rollers and line them up, overlapping slightly on a well-oiled pizza pan. Smooth out the seams, prick the crust with a fork, and then use as directed in your recipe.

Multigrain Crust

Multigrain and "ancient" grain flours are experiencing a surge in popularity — there's no shortage of varieties available. They normally cost a bit more and need to be stored in the refrigerator, but are full of whole grains and healthy fats.

Makes crust for four 12-inch pizzas

Ingredients
2 packages active dry yeast

1½ cups warm water, about 100°F

2 tablespoons honey

1 teaspoon sugar

1½ teaspoons salt

3½ cups bread flour

3 cups multigrain flour mix

2 tablespoons olive oil

1. In a large measuring cup, dissolve yeast in water. Let stand 5 minutes or until bubbly. Add honey to liquid. Combine sugar, salt, and both flours in the bowl of a mixer with a dough hook. Or, to mix by hand, place in a large bowl. Make a well in the flour mixture and pour in the water, followed by 1 tablespoon of oil.

2. Turn the mixer on low to blend, or begin stirring the flour into the liquid with a wooden spoon, a little at a time. When ingredients are well combined, turn the

mixer on medium-low to knead for 5 minutes. If working dough by hand, turn the dough onto a well-floured work surface. Use a pressing motion with the heels of your hands to push and stretch the dough. Work dough until mixture is slightly shiny and not too sticky to the touch.

3. The kneaded dough should be divided into four equal pieces. Store any dough not being used in a resealable bag in the refrigerator. Oil remaining dough and place in a bowl, covered, to rise for 1 hour. Punch the dough down, shape into two disks, and let rest for 30 minutes.

4. Grab dough by the edges, turning the disk a few inches at a time, allowing gravity to stretch the dough without tearing. Roll the dough into a crust shape or press into a pizza pan. Top as directed in recipe.

No-Yeast Crust

No time to let your dough rise? No yeast in your cupboard? Not to worry. You can still make great dough using this simple, foolproof recipe.

Makes crust for four 12-inch pizzas

Ingredients
5 cups all-purpose flour
1 cup vegetable shortening
1½ teaspoons salt
½ cup ice-cold water
1 egg, beaten

1. In a large bowl, pour flour and whisk to break up any lumps. Add shortening and salt to the bowl and work ingredients together with two knives or a pastry blender. Continue cutting and blending until mixture resembles pea-sized granules.

2. Add cold water and egg to the mixture and stir. Work with hands until mixture is well blended and holds together in a ball. Divide ball into four equal portions.

3. On a well-floured surface, roll each portion into a circle large enough to cover the bottom and sides of a 12" pizza or tart pan. (If you aren't making four pizzas, place any extra dough in resealable plastic bags and

refrigerate for later use.) Use pizza crust as directed in recipe.

Spinach Crust

If you can locate spinach flour at a specialty market, substitute up to a cup of bread flour in this recipe with it. Or follow the recipe as written and end up with a delicious veggie-flavored crust.

Makes crust for four 12-inch pizzas

Ingredients

2 packages active dry yeast

1½ cups warm water, about 100°F

1 teaspoon sugar

1½ teaspoons salt

7 cups bread flour

1 pound fresh spinach, lightly steamed

1 teaspoon lemon zest

⅛ teaspoon ground nutmeg

2 tablespoons olive oil

1. In a large measuring cup, dissolve yeast in water. Let stand 5 minutes or until bubbly. Combine sugar, salt, and bread flour in the bowl of a mixer with a dough hook. Or, to mix by hand, place in a large bowl. Make a well in the flour mixture and pour in the water, followed by 1 tablespoon of oil.

2. Squeeze as much liquid as possible from the spinach. Finely chop spinach by hand or with a food processor. Mix chopped spinach with lemon zest and nutmeg.

13

3. Turn the mixer on low to blend, or begin stirring the flour into the liquid with a wooden spoon, a little at a time. When ingredients are almost completely combined, add the spinach mixture and continue mixing.

4. When the spinach has been incorporated, turn the mixer on medium-low to knead for 5 minutes. If working dough by hand, turn the dough onto a well-floured work surface. Use a pressing motion with the heels of your hands to push and stretch the dough. Work dough until mixture is slightly shiny and not too sticky to the touch.

5. The kneaded dough should be divided into four equal pieces. Store any dough not being used in a resealable bag in the refrigerator. Oil remaining dough and place in a bowl, covered, to rise for 1 hour. Punch the dough down, shape into two disks, and let rest for 30 minutes.

6. Grab dough by the edges, turning slowly, allowing gravity to stretch the dough without tearing. Roll the dough into a crust shape or press into a pizza pan. Top as directed in recipe.

Grilling Pizza Crust

The mix of flours in this recipe gives the crust added texture and helps it stand up to the heat and smoke flavors of the grill.

Makes crust for four 12-inch pizzas

Ingredients
2 packages active dry yeast

1½ cups warm water, about 100°F

1 teaspoon sugar

1½ teaspoons salt

5 cups bread flour

1 cup semolina flour

½ cup whole-wheat or rye flour

2 tablespoons olive oil

1. In a large measuring cup, dissolve yeast in water. Let stand 5 minutes or until bubbly. Combine sugar, salt, and all flours in the bowl of a mixer with a dough hook. Or, to mix by hand, place in a large bowl. Make a well in the flour mixture and pour in the water, followed by 1 tablespoon of oil.

2. Turn the mixer on low to blend, or begin stirring the flour into the liquid with a wooden spoon, a little at a time. When ingredients are well combined, turn the mixer on medium-low to knead for 5 minutes. If working dough by hand, turn the dough onto a well-

floured work surface. Use a pressing motion with the heels of your hands to push and stretch the dough. Work dough until mixture is slightly shiny and not too sticky to the touch.

3. The kneaded dough should be divided into four equal pieces. Store any dough not being used in a resealable bag in the refrigerator. Oil remaining dough and place in a bowl, covered, to rise for 1 hour. Punch the dough down, shape into two disks, and let rest for 30 minutes.

4. Grab dough by the edges, turning the disk a few inches at a time, allowing gravity to stretch the dough without tearing. Roll the dough into a crust shape or press into a pizza pan. Top as directed in recipe.

Practice Makes Perfect (Pizza)

While it may seem like "everybody" is making grilled pizza, the truth is that the technique requires a bit of practice. If you'd like to start slowly, try grilling your pie indoors on an electric breakfast griddle or heavy stovetop grill pan. Cook the crust on both sides, turning once, then top and slide into the oven to finish.

Sweetie Pie Crust

Dessert pizzas make for such a fun ending to any meal! Add a dash of cinnamon, cocoa, or orange zest depending on how you plan on topping your pie.

Makes crust for four 12-inch pizzas

Ingredients
2 packages active dry yeast
1½ cups warm water, about 100°F
⅓ cup sugar
1½ teaspoons salt
7 cups bread flour
2 tablespoons softened butter
1 egg, beaten
2 teaspoons vanilla

1. In a large measuring cup, dissolve yeast in water. Let stand 5 minutes or until bubbly. Combine sugar, salt, and bread flour in the bowl of a mixer with a dough hook. Or, to mix by hand, place in a large bowl. Make a well in the flour mixture and pour in the water, followed by the butter, egg, and vanilla.

2. Turn the mixer on low to blend, or begin stirring the flour into the liquid with a wooden spoon, a little at a time. When ingredients are well combined, turn the mixer on medium-low to knead for 5 minutes. If

working dough by hand, turn the dough onto a well-floured work surface. Use a pressing motion with the heels of your hands to push and stretch the dough. Work dough until mixture is slightly shiny and not too sticky to the touch.

3. The kneaded dough should be divided into four equal pieces. Store any dough not being used in a resealable bag in the refrigerator. Place remaining dough in a bowl, covered, to rise for 1 hour. Punch the dough down, shape into two disks, and let rest for 30 minutes.

4. Roll the dough into a crust shape or press into a pizza pan. Top as directed in recipe.

Sweet Treats

Dessert pizzas are a fairly new phenomenon, but the concept is as old as Danish pastries. Essentially, you're pairing a pastry or sweet roll crust with such toppings as fruit, cream, chocolate, dessert cheese, nuts, and custard. Come up with your own signature dessert pizza and wow your guests.

Slow-Cooked Tomato Sauce

Prepare this basic, all-purpose pizza sauce in large batches and freeze in small containers for later use.

Makes 3 cups

Ingredients

1 tablespoon olive oil

6 ounces tomato paste

1 (29-ounce) can tomato sauce

4 cloves garlic, pressed

1 small onion, finely chopped

1 teaspoon sugar

1 teaspoon dried oregano

½ teaspoon dried basil

Pinch thyme

1 teaspoon red pepper flakes

Salt to taste

2 cups water

1. In a large kettle over medium-high heat, combine olive oil and tomato paste. Cook, stirring with a wooden spoon, for 2 minutes. Add tomato sauce and stir to dissolve paste in the sauce.

2. Add remaining ingredients. Bring to boil, then reduce heat to medium and simmer for 2 to 3 hours, stirring often. Cooked sauce should be reduced and thick.

19

Presto Pesto Sauce

A perfect project for when basil is growing in abundance, blend up large batches and freeze in ice cube trays. That way, you can just pop a pesto cube out when you want to spread it on your pie later.

Makes 2 cups

Ingredients
2½ cups fresh basil leaves
6 cloves garlic, chopped
⅔ cup pine nuts
⅔ cup grated Parmesan cheese
¼ cup grated Romano cheese
⅔ cup extra virgin olive oil

1. Combine basil, garlic, pine nuts, and cheeses in a food processor fitted with a metal blade. Pulse to finely chop ingredients.

2. With processor running, add olive oil to ingredients in a steady stream. Continue processing just until mixture is completely puréed and blended.

BBQ Sauce

Not for the faint of heart, this tangy and powerful sauce will leave you puckering!

Makes 3 cups

Ingredients
2 tablespoons vegetable oil

1 large onion, finely chopped

1 small green bell pepper, cored and chopped

3 cloves garlic, minced

3 tablespoons balsamic vinegar

Juice of 1 large lemon

1 tablespoon country Dijon mustard

2 tablespoons Worcestershire sauce

½ cup brown sugar

4 strips bacon, cooked

2⅓ cups ketchup

½ cup water

Tabasco sauce to taste

1. In a large saucepan over medium-high heat, combine oil, onion, bell pepper, and garlic. Sauté for 3 to 4 minutes until vegetables begin to soften. Spoon into a blender. Add remaining ingredients and pulse to purée.

2. Return sauce mixture to the saucepan. Bring to a boil over medium-high heat, stirring constantly. Reduce heat to medium-low and simmer for 1½ hours, stirring often. Cool before using in pizza recipes.

Creamy Cheesy Sauce

A variation on a classic Alfredo, this sauce makes a rich backdrop for vegetable and seafood pizzas. Leftover sauce can be thinned with light cream or broth and used to dress pasta.

Makes 3 cups

Ingredients
⅓ cup butter
4 cloves garlic, pressed
1 tablespoon finely minced green onion
1⅓ cups heavy cream
1¼ cups shredded Parmesan cheese
¼ cup shredded Romano cheese
Salt and freshly ground black pepper to taste

1. In a heavy saucepan, melt butter over medium heat. Whisk in garlic and green onion and cook, stirring constantly, for 2 minutes. Slowly whisk in heavy cream. Cook until cream is hot and just starting to bubble at the edges of the pan.

2. Add Parmesan and Romano cheeses, a small amount at a time, whisking until cheese has melted. Add salt and pepper to taste and remove from heat. Cool slightly, then use in pizza recipes.

Garlic Sauce

More of a garlic-infused oil than a traditional sauce, this fragrant
pizza topping will draw out the flavors of anything that tops it.
Closely monitor while cooking so the garlic doesn't burn!

Makes 2 cups

Ingredients
2 cups extra virgin olive oil
20 cloves garlic, minced
1 tablespoon minced fresh parsley
½ teaspoon red pepper flakes

1. In a saucepan or skillet, warm the olive oil over medium-low heat. Add garlic, parsley, and red pepper flakes. Cook, stirring often, for 4 to 5 minutes or until garlic has softened.

2. Remove from heat and cool slightly before using in recipes. Excess sauce can be tossed with pasta and Parmesan or refrigerated for later use.

Spinach Sauce

You can make this a nutrient-dense "green" sauce by adding other finely chopped, cooked veggies to the mix — try kale, broccoli, watercress, or another of your favorites.

Makes 3½ cups

Ingredients
¼ cup butter
4 cloves garlic, pressed
1 tablespoon finely minced green onion
1 cup heavy cream
1¼ cups shredded Parmesan cheese
1½ cups steamed spinach, drained
Salt and freshly ground black pepper to taste
Pinch nutmeg

1. In a heavy saucepan over medium heat, melt butter. Add garlic and green onion and cook, stirring constantly, for 2 minutes. Whisk in heavy cream and cook until simmering.

2. Whisk in Parmesan cheese, a little at a time, whisking until melted. Squeeze spinach to remove as much moisture as possible. Finely chop and add to the sauce along with salt, pepper, and nutmeg. Remove from heat. Cool slightly before using in pizza recipes.

Popeye's Passion

Iron-rich spinach is a low-calorie, high-flavor food and a good source of disease-fighting carotenoids and folate. Raw spinach should be purchased when leaves are fully green and spongy. To cook, rinse spinach well to remove sand and grit, then simply place in a covered pot over medium heat for a few minutes. The high water content of the greens makes added water unnecessary. Cooking reduces spinach volume by as much as three-fourths.

Creamy Lemon Sauce

Sauce flour sounds like what it is — a super fine white flour that takes the hassle out of making sauce. Because this sauce is very rich, it's best not to pair it with heavy meats and cheeses.

Makes 3 cups

Ingredients

¼ cup butter

2 tablespoons sauce flour

⅓ cup white wine

2 tablespoons fresh-squeezed lemon juice

1 teaspoon grated lemon zest

4 cloves garlic, pressed

1 tablespoon finely minced fresh parsley or dill

2 cups heavy cream

1 cup shredded Parmesan cheese

Salt and freshly ground black pepper to taste

1. In a heavy saucepan over medium heat, melt butter. Add sauce flour and cook, stirring, for 2 minutes. Add wine and lemon juice and whisk until smooth. Bring to a boil. Whisk in lemon zest, garlic, and herbs and cook for 2 minutes.

2. Turn heat to low. Slowly whisk cream into the mixture and cook just until hot but not simmering. Add Parmesan cheese to the sauce and remove from heat.

Stir occasionally. Once cheese has melted, use sauce in recipes.

Cook's Note

Once the cream has been whisked into the sauce, do not allow the mixture to boil and do not attempt to reheat the sauce.

Classic Cheese Pizza

Kids and adults alike will rejoice when you make a homemade version of the original pizza pie. Splurge on good-quality cheese and add a few slivers of fresh basil if the mood strikes.

Makes two 12-inch pizzas
∾

Ingredients
½ recipe <u>Classic Crust</u> dough
2 tablespoons cornmeal or 1 tablespoon olive oil
1½ cups <u>Slow-Cooked Tomato Sauce</u>
1 cup shredded Parmesan cheese
3 cups shredded mozzarella cheese

1. Roll or press pizza dough into two 12-inch circles, slightly thicker at the edges than in the center. If using pizza pans, sprinkle the bottom with cornmeal or coat with olive oil and place dough in pan. If using a pizza stone, sprinkle with cornmeal and place stone in oven. Preheat oven to 400°F.

2. Spread ¾ cup sauce in the center of each pizza, leaving at least an inch around the edges bare.

3. Sprinkle ½ cup Parmesan over the sauce on each pizza. Distribute 1½ cups mozzarella evenly over each pizza, just covering the sauce.

4. If using a hot stone or tiles, use a well-floured pizza peel to carefully lift one pizza from preparation surface and place on stone. If using pizza pans, place first pizza in the center of the oven. Bake for 15 to 20 minutes or until the crust is lightly browned and cheese is melted.

5. Remove pizza from oven carefully (use peel if baking with a stone). Set aside to rest briefly before slicing. Repeat baking process with second pie.

White Pizza

Too many slices of this rich pizza might not sit well with some folks, so this lends itself to being divvied into small pieces and passed as an appetizer. You can even provide dipping sauces — get creative!

Makes two 12-inch pizzas

Ingredients
½ recipe California Thin Crust dough

2 tablespoons cornmeal or 1 tablespoon oil

2 cloves garlic, pressed

½ cup extra virgin olive oil

¼ teaspoon kosher salt

1 cup shredded mozzarella cheese

½ cup shredded Parmesan cheese

½ cup shredded Asiago cheese

1. Roll or press pizza dough into two very thin 12-inch circles, slightly thicker at the edges than in the center. If using pizza pans, sprinkle the bottom with cornmeal or coat with oil and place dough in pan. If using a pizza stone, sprinkle with cornmeal and place rolled dough directly on stone.

2. Whisk pressed garlic into olive oil. Spread olive oil evenly over each pizza. Sprinkle each with kosher salt.

3. In a large bowl, combine all the cheeses and toss gently to mix. Sprinkle half the cheese blend over the oil on each pizza.

4. Place one pizza in the oven at 425°F. Bake 10 to 12 minutes or until crust is browned and cheese is melted. Repeat with remaining pizza.

5. Let pizzas rest briefly, then slice with a sharp knife or pizza wheel.

Pine Nut Pizza

The combination of pine nuts, Garlic Sauce, and basil give this a flavor that's slightly reminiscent of pesto, but the addition of Brie and Gruyère make it truly original.

Makes two 12-inch pizzas
꙳

Ingredients
½ recipe <u>Pan Pizza Crust</u> dough
2 tablespoons olive oil
2 tablespoons cornmeal
⅓ cup <u>Garlic Sauce</u>
3 cups grape tomatoes, halved lengthwise
1 cup toasted pine nuts
1 pound Brie, rind removed, diced
¼ cup fresh basil leaves
1 cup shredded Gruyère cheese

1. Roll out two circles of dough. Coat pans with olive oil and sprinkle with cornmeal. Place dough circles in the pans and press dough up the sides.

2. Divide Garlic Sauce over the two pizzas and spread over the bottom of the crust.

3. Spread 1½ cups of halved grape tomatoes over each crust, followed by ½ cup of pine nuts. Divide Brie between the two pizzas and distribute evenly over the

33

crusts. Sprinkle fresh basil leaves and ½ cup of Gruyère cheese over each pizza.

4. Preheat oven to 400°F. Bake pizzas until crust is light brown and cheese is melted and bubbly, about 15 to 20 minutes.

Greek Pizza

A slice of the Mediterranean on your plate. If you're craving more greens, include some fresh arugula as an additional topping.

Makes two 12-inch pizzas

Ingredients

½ recipe Spinach Crust dough
2 tablespoons cornmeal or 1 tablespoon olive oil
1½ cups Slow-Cooked Tomato Sauce
1½ cups shredded mozzarella cheese
2 cups crumbled feta cheese
1 cup chopped kalamata olives
¼ cup fresh oregano leaves
Black pepper to taste

1. Roll or press pizza dough into two 12-inch circles, slightly thicker at the edges than in the center. If using pizza pans, sprinkle the bottom with cornmeal or coat with olive oil and place dough in pan. If using a pizza stone, sprinkle with cornmeal and place stone in oven. Preheat oven to 400°F.

2. Spread ¾ cup sauce in the center of each pizza, leaving one inch around the edges bare.

3. Sprinkle ¾ cup mozzarella cheese over the sauce on each pizza. Distribute 1 cup crumbled feta evenly over

each pizza, leaving edges bare. Evenly distribute olives and oregano leaves, then grind black pepper to taste over each pizza.

4. If using a hot stone or tiles, use a well-floured pizza peel to carefully lift one pizza from preparation surface and place on stone. If using pizza pans, place first pizza in the center of the oven. Bake for 15 to 20 minutes or until the crust is lightly browned and cheese is melted.

5. Remove pizza from oven carefully (use peel if baking with a stone). Set aside to rest briefly before slicing. Repeat baking process with second pie.

More on Mozzarella

Adding mozzarella to specialty cheese pizzas like feta and Gorgonzola gives the pie more cheesy taste and texture without making the flavor overwhelming. If you're a hard-core pungent cheese fan, by all means, up the proportion of your favorite variety.

Cheesecake Pizza

Creamy and decadent, this pie tastes great on its own, but also pairs nicely with something relatively sweet and crunchy like sliced pears.

Makes two 12-inch pizzas

Ingredients
1 recipe No-Yeast Crust dough

1 tablespoon olive oil

½ cup Presto Pesto Sauce

2 pounds cream cheese

6 ounces goat cheese

½ cup sour cream

6 eggs

1 cup shredded mozzarella cheese

Black pepper to taste

1. Divide dough into two portions and roll into 12-inch circles. Oil two 12" tart pans and press dough into the pans and up the sides. Put nonstick foil over center of crust and fill with dried beans or pie weights. Bake at 350°F for 10 minutes. Remove from oven, remove foil, and let crusts cool slightly.

2. Brush insides of tart shells with Presto Pesto Sauce.

3. In a large bowl, combine cream cheese, goat cheese, and sour cream. Beat with an electric mixer on

medium speed until creamy. Add eggs one at a time, beating each until completely incorporated.

4. Pour cheesecake batter into tart pans and sprinkle shredded mozzarella over each. Grind black pepper to taste over each tart.

5. Bake pies for 30 minutes at 350°F or until center is set. Serve at room temperature.

Popeye Pizza with Artichokes

Artichokes from the can will work in this recipe. To really amplify the Popeye effect, use the Spinach Pizza Crust instead of the Pan Pizza Crust!

Makes two 12-inch pizzas

∾

Ingredients

½ recipe Pan Pizza Crust dough

2 tablespoons olive oil

2 cups Creamy Cheesy Sauce

2 pounds spinach leaves, stemmed and washed

1 teaspoon minced garlic

1 tablespoon butter

3 cups coarsely chopped cooked artichoke bottoms

1½ cups Parmesan cheese

2½ cups mozzarella cheese

Freshly ground black pepper

1. Roll pizza dough into two circles large enough to cover bottom and sides of two 12" pizza or quiche pans. Spread a tablespoon of olive oil over the bottom of each pan, then press dough circles into the pans.

2. Ladle 1 cup of sauce into each pan and spread evenly over the crust.

3. In a large, flat-bottomed wok or Dutch oven, combine washed spinach leaves, garlic, and butter. Sauté just until spinach has wilted. Remove spinach to a fine sieve and press out as much liquid as possible.

4. Distribute cooked spinach evenly over each pizza crust, then sprinkle artichokes evenly over the spinach.

5. Spread Parmesan cheese over each pizza, then do the same with the mozzarella. Add freshly ground black pepper to taste. Bake pans in a preheated oven at 400°F until crust has browned and cheese is bubbly, about 20 minutes.

Butterkase Pizza

Butterkase cheese is a mild, semisoft cheese that comes in both smoked and regular versions. If you can't locate it, Fontina works as a substitution.

Makes two 12-inch pizzas

Ingredients
½ recipe <u>California Thin Crust</u> dough
2 tablespoons cornmeal or 1 tablespoon oil
1 cup <u>Creamy Lemon Sauce</u>
¼ cup chopped fresh parsley
1 pound thinly sliced Butterkase cheese
1 pound blanched asparagus spears, trimmed
Freshly ground black pepper to taste

1. Roll pizza dough into two circles large enough to cover bottom and sides of two 12" pizza or quiche pans. Spread a tablespoon of olive oil over the bottom of each pan, and then press dough circles into the pans.

2. Ladle 1 cup of sauce into each pan and spread evenly over the crust.

3. In a large, flat-bottomed wok or Dutch oven, combine washed spinach leaves, garlic, and butter. Sauté just

until spinach has wilted. Remove spinach to a fine sieve and press out as much liquid as possible.

4. Distribute cooked spinach evenly over each pizza crust, and then sprinkle artichokes evenly over the spinach.

5. Spread Parmesan cheese over each pizza, and then do the same with the mozzarella. Add freshly ground black pepper to taste. Bake pans in a preheated oven at 400°F until crust has browned and cheese is bubbly, about 20 minutes.

Pick a Peck

Almost any vegetable can become the star attraction on a pizza, although some slow-cooking veggies should be blanched first. Try topping a white pizza with thinly sliced parboiled potatoes, drizzled with oil and garlic and topped with plenty of fresh herbs and a cheese blend.

Ratatouille Pie

Because this is filled with the Provencal flavors of Southern France nestled in a deep crust, it almost feels more like a tart than a pizza! Either way, it's delicious.

Makes two 12-inch pizzas

Ingredients
½ recipe <u>Pan Pizza Crust</u> dough
2 tablespoons olive oil
1 cup <u>Garlic Sauce</u>
1 cup diced zucchini
1 cup diced yellow squash
1 cup coarsely chopped white mushrooms
1 cup diced Japanese eggplant
2 cups diced fresh plum tomatoes
2 tablespoons fresh oregano leaves
Salt and pepper to taste
1 cup shredded Asiago cheese
1 cup shredded Parmesan cheese
2 cups shredded mozzarella cheese

1. Roll pizza dough into two circles large enough to cover bottom and sides of two 12" pizza or quiche pans. Spread a tablespoon of olive oil over the bottom of each pan, then press dough circles into the pans.

43

2. Spread ½ cup sauce over the bottom of each pie crust. In a bowl, combine zucchini, squash, mushrooms, eggplant, and tomatoes. Distribute vegetables evenly over each crust. Sprinkle with oregano leaves, salt, and pepper.

3. Combine Asiago, Parmesan, and mozzarella cheeses. Distribute evenly over the top of each pizza.

4. Bake pies at 400°F for 20 minutes or until browned and bubbly. Let stand for 5 minutes before serving.

Frijoles Pizza

Here you get a Mexican-inspired pie that is easy to assemble and easy on the wallet (if you use canned beans and frozen corn).

Makes two 12-inch pizzas
⟋⟍

Ingredients
½ recipe <u>Classic Crust</u> dough

2 tablespoons cornmeal or 1 tablespoon olive oil

1½ cups picante sauce

½ cup shredded Manchego cheese

1 cup shredded Cheddar cheese

2 cups shredded Monterey jack cheese

½ cup shredded mozzarella cheese

2 cups cooked black beans, drained

2 cups roasted corn kernels

1 bell pepper, cored and diced

1 small red onion, finely chopped

¼ cup minced cilantro

1. Roll or press pizza dough into two 12-inch circles, slightly thicker at the edges than in the center. If using pizza pans, sprinkle the bottom with cornmeal or coat with olive oil and place dough in pan. If using a pizza stone, sprinkle with cornmeal and place stone in oven. Preheat oven to 400°F.

2. Spread ¾ cup sauce in the center of each pizza, leaving edges bare.

3. In a large bowl, combine all the cheeses and toss gently to mix. Sprinkle half the cheese blend over the sauce on each pizza, leaving edges bare.

4. Divide black beans, corn, bell pepper, and onion evenly over each pizza. Sprinkle with minced cilantro.

5. If using a hot stone or tiles, use a well-floured pizza peel to carefully lift one pizza from preparation surface and place on stone. If using pizza pans, place first pizza in the center of the oven. Bake for 15 to 20 minutes or until the crust is lightly browned and cheese is melted.

6. Remove pizza from oven carefully (use peel if baking with a stone). Set aside to rest briefly before slicing. Repeat baking process with second pie.

Maui Wowie Hawaiian Pizza

Hawaiian pizza typically features ham and pineapple, but in this inspired rendition, grilled chicken takes the place of the pork.

Makes two 12-inch pizzas

Ingredients

½ recipe Classic Crust dough

2 tablespoons cornmeal or 1 tablespoon olive oil

2 cups Slow-Cooked Tomato Sauce

1 tablespoon brown sugar

1 tablespoon soy sauce

2 cups shredded Colby cheese

2 cups shredded mozzarella cheese

2 cups diced grilled or pan-seared chicken breast

1 cup diced green bell pepper

1 cup diced fresh or canned pineapple

½ cup diced red onion

¼ cup minced parsley

1. Roll or press pizza dough into two 12-inch circles, slightly thicker at the edges than in the center. If using pizza pans, sprinkle the bottom with cornmeal or coat with olive oil and place dough in pan. If using a pizza stone, sprinkle with cornmeal and place stone in oven. Preheat oven to 400°F.

2. In a bowl, combine tomato sauce, brown sugar, and soy sauce. Whisk to blend. Spread half the sauce in the center of each pizza, leaving edges bare.

3. Sprinkle 1 cup Colby over the sauce on each pizza. Distribute 1 cup mozzarella evenly over each pizza, leaving one inch around the edges bare.

4. Dot each pizza with 1 cup diced chicken breast, followed by ½ cup bell pepper and ½ cup pineapple. Sprinkle onion and parsley over each pizza.

5. If baking on a hot stone or tiles, use a well-floured pizza peel to carefully lift one pizza from preparation surface and place on stone. If using pizza pans, place first pizza in the center of the oven. Bake for 15 to 20 minutes or until the crust is lightly browned and toppings are bubbly.

6. Remove pizza from oven carefully (use peel if baking with a stone). Set aside to rest briefly before slicing. Repeat baking process with second pie.

BBQ Chicken Pizza

With premade crust and premade sauce all you need to do is pick up a roasted chicken on your way home or pull out leftovers and assemble this filling and crowd-pleasing pie.

Makes two 12-inch pizzas
༄

Ingredients
½ recipe Classic Crust dough

2 tablespoons cornmeal or 1 tablespoon olive oil

2 cups BBQ Sauce

2 cups shredded Cheddar or Colby cheese

2 cups shredded Monterey jack cheese

3 cups shredded roasted or poached chicken

⅓ cup sliced green onion

1. Roll or press pizza dough into two 12-inch circles, slightly thicker at the edges than in the center. If using pizza pans, sprinkle the bottom with cornmeal or coat with olive oil and place dough in pan. If using a pizza stone, sprinkle with cornmeal and place stone in oven. Preheat oven to 400°F.

2. Spread ¾ cup BBQ Sauce in the center of each pizza, leaving edges bare.

3. Sprinkle 1 cup Cheddar or Colby over the sauce on each pizza. Distribute 1 cup Monterey jack evenly over each pizza, leaving edges bare.

4. Toss remaining ½ cup BBQ Sauce with shredded chicken. Spread chicken evenly over the cheese on each pizza. Sprinkle sliced green onions over each pizza.

5. If using a hot stone or tiles, use a well-floured pizza peel to carefully lift one pizza from preparation surface and place on stone. If using pizza pans, place first pizza in the center of the oven. Bake for 15 to 20 minutes or until the crust is lightly browned and toppings are bubbly.

6. Remove pizza from oven carefully (use peel if baking with a stone). Set aside to rest briefly before slicing. Repeat baking process with second pie.

Alfredo's Delight Pizza

You can always reduce the amount of additional cheese on this pizza if the cheesy sauce is enough. Instead, layer some fresh spinach and some additional wild mushrooms to help fill the deep dish crust.

Makes two 12-inch pizzas

Ingredients
½ recipe <u>Pan Pizza Crust</u> dough
2 tablespoons olive oil
2 cups <u>Creamy Cheesy Sauce</u>
3 chicken breast halves, poached and diced
1 teaspoon minced garlic
1 tablespoon butter
2 cups coarsely chopped white mushrooms
1½ cups Parmesan cheese
2½ cups mozzarella cheese
Freshly ground black pepper

1. Roll pizza dough into two circles large enough to cover bottom and sides of two 12" pizza or quiche pans. Spread a tablespoon of olive oil over the bottom of each pan, then press dough circles into the pans.

2. Ladle 1 cup of sauce into each pan and spread evenly over the crust. Divide diced chicken and distribute over each pizza.

51

3. In a large, flat-bottomed wok or Dutch oven, combine garlic, butter, and mushrooms. Sauté 3 to 5 minutes or until mushrooms soften. Remove mushrooms with a slotted spoon and spread over chicken.

4. Spread Parmesan cheese over each pizza, then do the same with the mozzarella. Add freshly ground black pepper to taste. Bake pans in a preheated oven at 400°F until crust has browned and cheese is bubbly, about 20 minutes.

Is Alfredo a Person or a Dish?

Both! Around 1914, Roman restaurateur Alfredo di Lelio created a dish of supremely thin, tender egg noodles, extra-rich butter, and freshly grated Parmesan cheese. He served it with a flourish, brandishing golden cutlery, and named it Fettuccine all'Alfredo. Eventually, the rest of the world began calling any white Parmesan sauce-laced dish "Alfredo." However, in Rome, the name still refers to a specific dish.

Crab Extravaganza

This decadent pizza requires a fork and knife to truly enjoy. Heat some tomato sauce and reserve as an option for dipping!

Makes two 12-inch pizzas

Ingredients

½ recipe California Thin Crust dough

2 tablespoons olive oil

2 tablespoons cornmeal

2 cups Spinach Sauce

2 cups shredded mozzarella cheese

1 pound lump crabmeat, rinsed and picked for shells

⅔ cup finely diced red bell pepper

¼ cup fresh basil ribbons

1 cup shredded Parmesan cheese

½ cup shredded Asiago cheese

1. Roll or press pizza dough into two thin 12-inch circles, slightly thicker at the edges than in the center. Spread 1 tablespoon olive oil over the bottom of two pizza pans or large quiche pans. Sprinkle cornmeal over the oil, 1 tablespoon on each pan.

2. Preheat oven to 400°F. Place pizza pans in the oven and prick in several places with a fork. Bake until crust is lightly browned, about 7 minutes. Remove from the

oven and spoon or brush 1 cup of Spinach Sauce over each pizza.

3. Divide mozzarella evenly over each pizza, followed by crabmeat, bell pepper, and basil ribbons.

4. Combine shredded Parmesan and Asiago cheeses. Sprinkle evenly over pizzas.

5. Return pizzas to the oven and bake until shredded cheese has melted and crusts darken slightly, about 5 to 7 minutes. Let pizzas rest briefly, then slice with a sharp knife or pizza wheel. If oven won't accommodate both pans easily, bake pizzas one at a time.

Shrimp and Artichoke Pizza

Sweet shrimp, tangy bright lemon sauce, and earthy-tart artichokes combine in this Pan Pizza Crust in a way that will wake up your taste buds. Expect no leftovers.

Makes two 12-inch pizzas

Ingredients

½ recipe <u>Pan Pizza Crust</u> dough

2 tablespoons olive oil

2 cups <u>Creamy Lemon Sauce</u>

2 pounds cooked shrimp, peeled and deveined

3 cups quartered cooked artichoke hearts

1½ cups Parmesan cheese

2½ cups mozzarella cheese

Freshly ground black pepper

1. Roll pizza dough into two circles large enough to cover bottom and sides of two 12" pizza or quiche pans. Spread a tablespoon of olive oil over the bottom of each pan, then press dough circles into the pans.

2. Ladle 1 cup of sauce into each pan and spread evenly over the crust.

3. Distribute cooked shrimp evenly over each pizza crust, then sprinkle artichokes evenly over the pizzas.

4. Spread Parmesan cheese over each pizza, then do the same with the mozzarella. Add black pepper to taste. Bake at 400°F until browned and bubbly, about 20 minutes.

Zesty Scallop Pizza

For moist scallops, just brown the top and bottom in a skillet. Don't cook them all the way through. They'll finish cooking on the pizzas.

Makes two 12-inch pizzas

Ingredients

½ recipe California Thin Crust dough

2 tablespoons cornmeal or 1 tablespoon oil

1 cup Garlic Sauce

1 cup shredded Manchego cheese

2 cups shredded mozzarella cheese

24 large scallops, briefly pan-seared

¼ cup minced fresh parsley

4 tablespoons grated lemon zest

Freshly ground black pepper to taste

1. Roll or press pizza dough into two very thin 12-inch circles, slightly thicker at the edges than in the center. If using pizza pans, sprinkle the bottom with cornmeal or coat with oil and place dough in pan. If using a pizza stone, sprinkle with cornmeal and place rolled dough directly on stone.

2. Spread ½ cup Garlic Sauce evenly over each pizza. Combine the cheeses and spread over the sauce.

3. Arrange a dozen scallops over each pizza and sprinkle the tops with parsley and lemon zest. Add pepper to taste.

4. Place one pizza in the oven at 425°F. Bake 10 to 12 minutes or until crust is browned and cheese is melted. Repeat with remaining pizza. Let pizzas rest briefly, then slice with a sharp knife or pizza wheel.

"Steak" Your Claim Pizza

Omit the diced tomatoes and instead include mushrooms and onions as a topping to turn this into a pizza that's reminiscent of a cheesesteak sub!

Makes two 12-inch pizzas

Ingredients
½ recipe Classic Crust dough

2 tablespoons cornmeal or 2 tablespoons olive oil

1½ cups Slow-Cooked Tomato Sauce

1½ cups shredded mozzarella cheese

1 cup shredded provolone cheese

1 pound very rare sirloin or New York strip steak, thinly sliced

2 cups diced plum tomatoes

1 cup crumbled bleu cheese

Freshly ground black pepper to taste

1. Roll or press pizza dough into two 12-inch circles, slightly thicker at the edges than in the center. If using pizza pans, sprinkle the bottom with cornmeal or coat with olive oil and place dough in pan. If using a pizza stone, sprinkle with cornmeal and place stone in oven. Preheat oven to 400°F.

2. Spread ¾ cup sauce in the center of each pizza, leaving one inch around the edges bare.

3. In a large bowl, combine mozzarella and provolone cheeses and toss gently to mix. Sprinkle half the cheese blend over the sauce on each pizza, leaving edges bare. Arrange steak strips in circular pattern over each pizza. Distribute tomatoes over each pizza, followed by crumbled bleu cheese and pepper.

4. If using a hot stone or tiles, use a well-floured pizza peel to carefully lift one pizza from preparation surface and place on stone. If using pizza pans, place first pizza in the center of the oven. Bake for 15 to 20 minutes or until the crust is lightly browned and cheese is melted.

5. Remove pizza from oven carefully (use peel if baking with a stone). Set aside to rest briefly before slicing. Repeat baking process with second pie.

Peppy Pepperoni Pizza

Seek out high-quality pepperoni and load up this pie! If you want the meat to get crispy, try not to overlap the slices.

Makes two 12-inch pizzas

Ingredients

½ recipe Classic Crust dough

2 tablespoons cornmeal or 1 tablespoon olive oil

1½ cups Slow-Cooked Tomato Sauce

1 cup shredded Parmesan cheese

3 cups shredded mozzarella cheese

8 ounces pepperoni, sliced

1. Roll or press pizza dough into two 12-inch circles, slightly thicker at the edges than in the center. If using pizza pans, sprinkle the bottom with cornmeal or coat with olive oil and place dough in pan. If using a pizza stone, sprinkle with cornmeal and place stone in oven. Preheat oven to 400°F.

2. Spread ¾ cup sauce in the center of each pizza, leaving one inch around the edges bare.

3. Sprinkle ½ cup Parmesan over the sauce on each pizza. Distribute 1½ cups mozzarella evenly over each pizza, leaving edges bare. Distribute pepperoni slices evenly over each pizza.

4. If baking on a hot stone or tiles, use a well-floured pizza peel to carefully lift one pizza from preparation surface and place on stone. If using pizza pans, place first pizza in the center of the oven. Bake for 15 to 20 minutes or until the crust is lightly browned and cheese is melted.

5. Remove pizza from oven carefully (use peel if baking with a stone). Set aside to rest briefly before slicing. Repeat baking process with second pie.

Passion for Pepperoni

Pepperoni is by far America's favorite pizza topping, accounting for more than a third of pizzas ordered. Pepperoni is a dry salami, made from beef, pork, veal, and spices. It's available in small- or large-diameter rolls and with varying levels of spiciness and moisture. Try several varieties to find your favorite.

Lebanon "No Bologna" Pizza

A smoky, intensely flavored Pennsylvania Dutch-country cold cut, Lebanon bologna bears little resemblance to standard deli bologna. Ask for it at your supermarket deli counter.

Makes two 12-inch pizzas

Ingredients
½ recipe Classic Crust dough

2 tablespoons cornmeal or 1 tablespoon olive oil

1½ cups Slow-Cooked Tomato Sauce

1½ cups shredded mozzarella cheese

1½ cups shredded Cheddar cheese

½ pound Lebanon bologna slices, quartered

1. Roll or press pizza dough into two 12-inch circles, slightly thicker at the edges than in the center. If using pizza pans, sprinkle the bottom with cornmeal or coat with olive oil and place dough in pan. If using a pizza stone, sprinkle with cornmeal and place stone in oven. Preheat oven to 400°F.

2. Spread ¾ cup sauce in the center of each pizza, leaving one inch around the edges bare.

3. Combine the mozzarella and Cheddar cheeses and toss gently to mix. Sprinkle half the cheese blend over

the sauce on each pizza, leaving edges bare. Distribute Lebanon bologna over the cheese.

4. If using a hot stone or tiles, use a well-floured pizza peel to carefully lift one pizza from preparation surface and place on stone. If using pizza pans, place first pizza in the center of the oven. Bake for 15 to 20 minutes or until the crust is lightly browned and cheese is melted.

5. Remove pizza from oven carefully. Use peel if baking with a stone. Set aside to rest briefly before slicing. Repeat baking process with second pie.

Prosciutto, Pear, and Gorgonzola Pie

There are few ingredients on this pizza, but each packs a strong, flavorful punch — salty, sweet, spicy, and pungent — that work together wonderfully.

Makes two 12-inch pizzas

Ingredients

½ recipe California Thin Crust dough

2 tablespoons cornmeal or 1 tablespoon oil

1 cup Garlic Sauce

2 small pears, peeled, cored, and sliced

4 ounces thinly sliced prosciutto

1 cup crumbled Gorgonzola cheese

1. Roll or press pizza dough into two very thin 12-inch circles, slightly thicker at the edges than in the center. If using pizza pans, sprinkle the bottom with cornmeal or coat with oil and place dough in pan. If using a pizza stone, sprinkle with cornmeal and place rolled dough directly on stone.

2. Spread Garlic Sauce evenly over each pizza. Arrange pear slices in a circular pattern over the pizzas. Cut prosciutto into slivers and spread over pear slices. Sprinkle Gorgonzola over the pizzas.

3. Place one pizza in the oven at 425°F. Bake 10 to 12 minutes or until crust is browned and cheese is soft. Repeat with remaining pizza.

4. Let pizzas rest briefly, then slice with a sharp knife or pizza wheel.

The Fruits of Your Labor

Firm fruits like apples, pears, and quince make a great addition to pizzas featuring smoky meats and intense cheeses. Be sure to slice fruits thinly enough that they soften slightly during baking. You probably want to remove the peels on most fruits, too, as the peels will dry up as the fruit cooks.

Kinda Sorta Homemade Pizza

No time to prepare your own pizza dough or sauce? No problem. With this formula you can have dinner on the table in a matter of minutes. Feel free to add toppings according to what's in your refrigerator.

Makes two 12-inch pizzas

Ingredients
2 shelf-stable 12-inch pizza crusts (Boboli or other)
1 cup jarred pizza sauce or thick pasta sauce
4 cups preshredded Italian six-cheese blend
2 cups sliced pepperoni

1. Place one ready-to-top crust on a perforated pizza pan or pizza stone. Spread half the sauce over the top of the pizza, leaving the edges of the crust bare. Sprinkle 2 cups cheese evenly over the sauce. Distribute 1 cup pepperoni slices over the cheese.

2. Bake at 450°F for 12 minutes or until cheese is melted and bubbly. Remove from oven and let rest briefly before slicing. Repeat procedure with remaining ingredients to make second pie.

Kick Back and Relax!
Yes, from scratch cooking yields many rewards — both psychic and gastronomic. But even if you don't have time to do it all yourself, you don't have to resort to take-out food. Supermarkets are full of products like ready-to-top pizza crusts, preshredded cheese, cooked meats, and prechopped veggies. In general, these items are higher quality than the cardboard-tasting versions of a decade ago.

Pepperoni Crust Pizza

The end result of this layered pie is more akin to a pepperoni lasagna than pizza! It's a meat lovers' favorite.

Makes two 9-inch pies

Ingredients

2 refrigerated pie crusts

1 pound mozzarella slices

2 cups thick pasta sauce

1 can chopped tomatoes, drained

2 cups sliced pepperoni

1 cup chopped pepperoni

1 cup shredded Parmesan cheese

1. Unfold pie crusts and press into two greased 9" deep-dish pie pans. Layer cheese slices over the crust. Combine pasta sauce and tomatoes and spoon a small amount over the cheese. Top with a layer of sliced pepperoni and chopped pepperoni.

2. Continue to layer cheese, sauce, and pepperoni in the pie crust, until all the ingredients have been used. Sprinkle Parmesan over the top of each pie.

3. Bake pies at 350°F for 30 minutes or until pies are browned and bubbly.

Deep Dish, Quick Dish

Ordinary pie crust can be used to create deep-dish pizzas. Or line a pie pan with refrigerated crescent roll or flattened biscuit dough for a springier crust. For a really unusual improvised crust, hollow out a round loaf of hearth-baked artisan bread. Fill it with a small amount of sauce, meats, and cheese and bake until the cheese is melted.

On-the-Go Pizza Pretzels

Pizza pretzels make for an excellent snack or quick bite if you lack time for a proper dinner. A bonus: they freeze well, so you can grab and go!

Makes 4 pizza pretzels

Ingredients
1 pound frozen bread dough, thawed

½ cup pizza sauce

1 teaspoon dried oregano

Red pepper flakes to taste

4 slices provolone cheese

4 slices mozzarella cheese

1. Allow bread dough to rise until doubled in size. Punch down and divide into four pieces. Roll each piece into a 20-inch rope. Line two baking sheets with nonstick foil. Coil dough ropes into four pretzels, two on each sheet. Let dough rise for about an hour.

2. Gently spoon pizza sauce over the pretzels and sprinkle each with oregano and, if desired, red pepper flakes. Bake at 400°F for 10 minutes or until pretzels are golden.

3. Immediately top each pretzel with a slice of provolone and a slice of mozzarella. Let stand until cheese melts over pretzels. Serve.

Ricotta and Spinach Turnovers

This delicious vegetarian calzone can easily serve a family of four. But if you're really hungry, throw some chopped sausage or chicken in to make it even more filling!

Makes two 12-inch-long turnovers
~

Ingredients

½ recipe <u>Grilling Pizza Crust</u> dough

Cornmeal and flour for dusting

Vegetable oil

1 cup <u>Slow-Cooked Tomato Sauce</u>

2 cups steamed spinach, squeezed dry and chopped

¼ cup minced green onion

1 egg, beaten

2 pounds ricotta cheese

Black pepper and salt to taste

¼ teaspoon dried oregano

2 cups shredded mozzarella cheese

1. On a lightly floured board or on parchment, roll out two 12-inch dough circles. Place each circle of dough on a metal pizza peel or rimless baking sheet generously sprinkled with flour and cornmeal.

2. In a large bowl, stir tomato sauce into chopped spinach and green onion until well mixed. Stir in beaten egg, then fold in ricotta cheese. Add black

71

pepper and salt to taste and stir in oregano. Fold mozzarella into the mixture. Spoon filling mixture onto one side of the dough circles, leaving dough edges bare. Divide mixture evenly. Carefully lift the dough from the uncovered side and lay it over the filling. Press the edges of the dough together to form a sealed turnover.

3. Prepare a gas or charcoal grill so the cooking surface is medium-hot. Brush the grill rack with vegetable oil. Slide the turnovers onto the grill rack over the hot coals or heating element. Close the lid immediately and grill for 3 to 4 minutes or until dough is cooked on the bottom and grill marks appear. Carefully flip the turnover over and cook the other side for 5 to 7 minutes. Remove from the grill and cool slightly before serving.

Hickory Fruit Pizza

*Serve this not-too-sweet pizza with wedges of Camembert, Port Salut,
Gouda, and Cheddar cheese for a unique cheese-course dish.*

Makes two 12-inch pizzas

Ingredients

½ recipe Grilling Pizza Crust dough
Cornmeal and flour for dusting
Vegetable oil
3 tablespoons melted butter
1 cup apricot preserves, warmed
2 cups sliced fresh peaches
1 cup sliced fresh plums
1 cup pitted fresh cherries
1 cup fresh blueberries
4 tablespoons brown sugar

1. On a lightly floured board or on parchment, roll out two 12-inch dough circles. Place one circle of dough on a metal pizza peel or rimless baking sheet generously sprinkled with flour and cornmeal.

2. Prepare a gas or charcoal grill so that one area is hot while another side or corner is medium-hot. Brush the grill rack with vegetable oil. Slide the pizza onto the grill rack over the hot coals or heating element. Close the lid immediately and grill for 2 to 3 minutes or until

pizza dough is cooked on the bottom and grill marks appear. Remove dough to peel or baking sheet, turning the grilled side up.

3. Brush the grilled pizza side with half the butter, then quickly spread half the apricot jam over the top. Cover the sauce with half the slices of peaches and plums, half the cherries, and half the blueberries. Sprinkle the fruit with 2 tablespoons brown sugar.

4. Carefully slide the pizza back onto the grill, placing it over the medium-hot area. Close grill cover and cook 3 minutes. Check to make sure crust isn't browning too quickly. If it is, move some coals to the opposite side of the grill or lower gas grill thermostat to reduce heat.

5. Continue to cook for another 4 to 5 minutes or until crust is browned and fruit is softened. Remove from heat, cool slightly, and serve. Repeat cooking process with second pizza.

Porcini Mushroom and Chicken Calzones

Porcini mushrooms are prized by gourmet chefs and are just as potent dried as they are fresh. If you can only find the former, reconstitute in water, drain, and add to the pizza. Shitakes are a good second choice.

Makes three 8-inch calzones

Ingredients

½ recipe <u>Classic Crust</u> dough

⅓ cup <u>Garlic Sauce</u>

3 cups shredded cooked chicken

3 green onions, minced

1 cup chopped porcini mushrooms

3 cups ricotta cheese

1 cup shredded mozzarella cheese

Salt and black pepper to taste

3 tablespoons cornmeal

1. Separate dough into three pieces. Place segments on a heavily floured work surface and roll each one into an 8-inch circle. Brush each circle with Garlic Sauce.

2. Combine shredded chicken, green onion, and mushrooms. Spread 1 cup of the ricotta onto half of each dough circle, leaving one inch around the edges bare. Distribute one-third of the chicken mixture over

the ricotta, followed by ⅓ cup mozzarella cheese. Season with salt and black pepper to taste.

3. Fold dough over the filling to form a crescent. Press dough edges together, brushing edges with a little water if necessary. Sprinkle cornmeal over a baking sheet or pizza tiles and place calzones on the cornmeal. Cover with a damp towel and let stand 1 hour.

4. With a sharp knife, cut two or three slits in the tops of the calzones. Bake at 375°F for 20 to 25 minutes. Remove from oven and let stand a few minutes before serving.

Muffaletta Turnovers

Omit or substitute any of the ingredients listed here and you'll need to change the name of these New Orleans-inspired calzones. Olive salad can be found in the deli section of your grocery.

Makes three 8-inch turnovers

Ingredients

½ recipe <u>Classic Crust</u> dough

½ cup <u>Garlic Sauce</u>

1⅓ cups olive salad, drained

½ cup chopped roasted red peppers

1 cup diced ham

1 cup diced salami

1 cup diced mortadella

3 cups diced provolone cheese

Black pepper to taste

3 tablespoons cornmeal

1. Separate dough into three pieces. Place segments on a heavily floured work surface and roll each one into an 8-inch circle. Spread one-third of the sauce over each circle.

2. Combine olive salad, peppers, ham, salami, mortadella, and provolone. Spoon one-third of the mixture onto half of each dough circle, leaving edges bare. Season with black pepper to taste.

3. Fold dough over the filling to form a crescent. Press dough edges together, brushing edges with a little water if necessary. Sprinkle cornmeal over a baking sheet or pizza tiles and place turnovers on the cornmeal. Cover with a damp towel and let stand 1 hour.

4. With a sharp knife, cut two or three slits in the tops of the turnovers. Bake at 375°F for 20 to 25 minutes. Remove from oven and let stand a few minutes before serving.

Muffa-What?

Central Grocery in the French Quarter of New Orleans is the home of the original Muffaletta sandwich, and it's still made at the grocery deli counter and wrapped in white paper. The sandwich, which has Sicilian roots, is made by splitting a large round loaf of crusty Italian bread and filling it with many layers of cured meats and cheeses. The crowning glory is a layer of olive salad that seeps into the bread and flavors the entire sandwich.

Party Pizza Canapés

Downsize your standard 12-inch pizza to make bite-size delicacies perfect for passing at your next cocktail party. Feel free to modify the sauces and toppings according to you and your guests' tastes.

Makes 24 canapés

Ingredients

½ recipe Classic Crust dough

3 tablespoons olive oil

1 cup Creamy Cheesy Sauce

1½ cup lump crabmeat

¼ cup minced parsley

1 cup Presto Pesto Sauce

12 large boiled shrimp, peeled

¼ cup minced basil

1. Divide dough in half, then break each half into twelve pieces. With fingers, flatten each bit into a tiny pizza crust. Line two baking sheets with nonstick foil. Place 12 dough circles on each baking sheet. Brush tops lightly with olive oil and bake at 350°F for 10 minutes or until lightly browned.

2. Allow crusts to cool. Spread twelve with Creamy Cheesy Sauce and top each of those with lump crabmeat. Sprinkle parsley on top and place six on each of two serving platters.

79

3. Spread remaining crusts with Presto Pesto Sauce. Place a shrimp in the center of each and sprinkle with minced basil. Place six on each serving platter and serve.

The Host with the Most

When hosting a party, try not to load all the food onto one table, forcing everyone to crowd around. Instead, encourage good party flow and mingling by creating several small islands of food — a tray here, a tray there. And never put the bar next to the main buffet.

"Two-Bites or Less" Mini Crab Pizzas

Mini pizzas spare you the effort of cutting and divvying up the pie! With this combo, traditional Italian flavors marry with crab legs to create an original treat.

Makes 24 mini-pizzas

Ingredients
½ recipe Classic Crust dough
3 tablespoons olive oil
1 cup Slow-Cooked Tomato Sauce
2 cups ricotta cheese
2 cups peeled, sliced crab legs
2 cups mozzarella cheese
⅓ cup fresh herbs

1. Divide dough in half, then break each half into twelve pieces. With fingers, flatten each bit into a tiny pizza crust. Line two baking sheets with nonstick foil. Place twelve dough circles on each baking sheet. Brush tops lightly with olive oil and bake at 350°F for 8 minutes.

2. Spread crusts with a small amount of tomato sauce and add a dollop of ricotta cheese. Divide crab legs over pizzas, then top with cheese and minced herbs.

Return to oven 3 to 5 minutes or until mozzarella melts. Place six on each serving platter and serve.

Straight from the Garden Pizza

Load on as many veggies as you can; the dense and delicious Multigrain Crust can withstand the weight. A pizza stone will help you achieve a crispy — and sturdy — bottom.

Makes two 12-inch pizzas

Ingredients
½ recipe Multigrain Crust dough
2 tablespoons cornmeal or 1 tablespoon olive oil
1½ cups Slow-Cooked Tomato Sauce
3 cups shredded part-skim mozzarella cheese
1 cup shredded sharp Cheddar cheese
1 cup diced yellow squash
1 cup diced plum tomatoes
1 cup chopped blanched broccoli
2 cups sliced mushrooms
1 small onion, sliced
1 small green bell pepper, cored and diced
¼ cup minced fresh basil

1. Roll or press pizza dough into two 12-inch circles, slightly thicker at the edges than in the center. If using pizza pans, sprinkle the bottom with cornmeal or coat with olive oil and place dough in pan. If using a pizza stone, sprinkle with cornmeal and place stone in oven. Preheat oven to 400°F.

2. Spread ¾ cup sauce in the center of each pizza, leaving one inch around the edges bare. Combine mozzarella and Cheddar cheeses and divide evenly over each pizza.

3. Layer squash, tomatoes, broccoli, mushrooms, onion, and bell pepper over the cheese. Sprinkle with fresh basil.

4. If using a hot stone or tiles, use a well-floured pizza peel to carefully lift one pizza from preparation surface and place on stone. If using pizza pans, place first pizza in the center of the oven. Bake for 15 to 20 minutes or until the crust is lightly browned and cheese is melted.

5. Remove pizza from oven carefully (use peel if baking with a stone). Set aside to rest briefly before slicing. Repeat baking process with second pie.

Mushroom Madness

Mushrooms are nature's sponges. Thinly sliced raw mushrooms will soften when baked on pizzas, releasing a tiny bit of flavorful broth as they cook. If you prefer, you can sauté mushrooms — and flavor them with oil, garlic, herbs, and wine — before adding them to your pizza.

Sizzling Salmon Turnovers

These turnovers feature heart-healthy salmon wrapped in a heart-healthy Multigrain Crust. The cheese, dill, and mushrooms combine to enhance the goodness.

Makes three 8-inch turnovers

Ingredients
½ recipe <u>Multigrain Crust</u> dough
3 tablespoons olive oil
2 cups part-skim ricotta cheese
3 cups flaked cooked salmon
3 green onions, minced
1 cup chopped mushrooms
¼ cup chopped fresh dill
1 cup shredded part-skim mozzarella cheese
Salt and black pepper to taste
3 tablespoons cornmeal

1. Separate dough into three pieces. Place segments on a heavily floured work surface and roll each one into an 8-inch circle. Brush each circle with olive oil.

2. Spread one-third of the ricotta onto half of each dough circle, leaving one inch around the edges bare. Combine the salmon, green onions, mushrooms, and dill. Distribute one-third of the salmon mixture over the ricotta on each circle, followed by ⅓ cup

mozzarella cheese. Season with salt and black pepper to taste.

3. Fold dough over the filling to form a crescent. Press dough edges together, brushing edges with a little water if necessary. Sprinkle cornmeal over a baking sheet or pizza tiles and place turnovers on the cornmeal. Cover with a damp towel and let stand 1 hour.

4. With a sharp knife, cut two or three slits in the tops of the turnovers. Bake at 375°F for 20 to 25 minutes. Remove from oven and let stand a few minutes before serving.

Get Savvy about Salmon

Wild Alaskan salmon costs a little more than the farmed variety, but it contains more of the Omega-3 fatty acids so prized for health benefits. Frozen wild salmon fillets and patties are available at large discount stores and are less expensive than fresh fillets.

Curry-Spiced Chicken Pizza

Omit the yogurt for a lactose-free pie, that surprises with spiciness and offbeat ingredients. Leftover chicken works well here, and if you're able to go with just-squeezed OJ, you'll appreciate the burst of fresh flavor.

Makes two 12-inch pizzas

Ingredients

2 large Vidalia onions, sliced

2 tablespoons peanut oil

1 clove garlic, minced

1 teaspoon curry powder

Pinch cayenne

1 tablespoon orange juice

1½ cups finely diced chicken breast

½ recipe Multigrain Crust dough

2 tablespoons cornmeal or 2 tablespoons olive oil

1 cup Slow-Cooked Tomato Sauce

1 cup plain yogurt (optional)

Freshly ground black pepper to taste

1. In a large skillet or Dutch oven, combine onions, peanut oil, and garlic. Cook over medium heat, stirring often, until onions turn a rich brown. Stir in curry powder, cayenne, and orange juice. Simmer for 1 minute, then add chicken and mix well.

2. Roll dough into two 12-inch circles, slightly thicker at the edges than in the center. If using pizza pans, sprinkle the bottom with cornmeal or coat with olive oil and place dough in pan. If using a pizza stone, sprinkle with cornmeal and place stone in oven. Preheat oven to 400°F.

3. Spread a thin layer of pizza sauce over each crust, leaving one inch around the edges bare. Divide the curry-spiced chicken mixture over the sauce on each pizza.

4. Bake pizzas, one at a time if necessary, at 400°F in the center of the oven for 15 minutes or until browned. Remove and let stand for 5 minutes, then slice and serve.

Fruity Shortcake Pie

This shortcake pie can serve as an elegant finish to a dinner party, or a fun way to stick with a theme at a kids' pizza party. Either way, this easy-to-assemble dessert will leave guests smiling!

Makes two 10-inch pizzas

Ingredients
2 large spongecake shells

4 cups fruit sauce

6 cups sweetened whipped cream

1 cup caramel sauce

24 whole strawberries

1. Place spongecake shells on serving platters. Carefully spread 2 cups strawberry fruit sauce over each shell. Allow sauce to cool.

2. Pile whipped cream over the sauce on each spongecake and drizzle caramel sauce over each. Garnish each with whole strawberries.

Fruit Sauce Shortcut

Make your fruit sauce with strawberries for this recipe. If you don't have time to make fruit sauce from scratch, just place coarsely chopped strawberries and a jar of strawberry jam in a saucepan and heat until melted and well blended.

Creamy Chocolate Pizza

This is a chocolate-lovers' dream pizza. Use graham crackers in place of the chocolate sandwich cookies and you've got a giant pie of S'mores.

Makes one 12-inch pizza

Ingredients
1 package brownie mix, plus ingredients to prepare
½ cup butter
1 cup marshmallow cream
3 cups confectioners' sugar
1 teaspoon vanilla
1 (18-ounce) package chocolate sandwich cookies

1. Prepare brownie batter according to package directions. Pour into a lightly greased pizza pan and bake 12 minutes or until set. Remove from oven and let cool completely.

2. Place butter and marshmallow cream in a medium bowl. Beat with a mixer on medium speed until creamy. Add confectioners' sugar and vanilla. Spread cream over brownie crust.

3. Place 12 whole cookies around the edges of the pizza. Break up the remaining cookies and sprinkle over the pizza. Serve with coffee or icy milk.

Not-Your-Typical Pineapple Pizza

Get a taste of the tropics with this unique and simple take on a pineapple upside-down cake.

Makes two 12-inch pizzas
∽

Ingredients
½ recipe <u>Sweetie Pie Crust</u> dough

3 tablespoons melted butter

2 cups brown sugar

24 fresh pineapple rings

1 cup pitted cherries

1 cup shredded coconut (optional)

1. Roll or press pizza dough into two 12-inch circles, slightly thicker at the edges than in the center. Coat each pizza pan with ½ tablespoon melted butter and place dough in the pans. Brush dough with remaining butter. Top each pizza with half the brown sugar. Layer 12 pineapple rings over each pizza and dot with half the cherries.

2. Bake pizzas at 375°F for 20 minutes. Remove from oven and let stand for a few minutes. Sprinkle with shredded coconut, if desired. Serve warm.

Pineapple 101

Fresh pineapple contains an enzyme that keeps gelatin from getting firm. The same enzyme, papain, is also found in papaya and it's often used as a meat tenderizer. To use pineapple in dishes thickened with gelatin, be sure to use canned pineapple. The cooking and canning process neutralizes the papain.

Fruit Pizza

A tart by any other name, this pizza can just as easily be loaded up with fresh berries or a cinnamony mixture of apples and pears. Go with what's seasonal, top with fresh whipped cream, and enjoy!

Makes two 12-inch pizzas

Ingredients
½ recipe Sweetie Pie Crust dough

2 tablespoons melted butter

1 cup sliced fresh peaches

1 cup sliced fresh nectarines

1 cup sliced fresh plums

1 cup pitted cherries

½ cup brown sugar

1. Roll or press pizza dough into two 12-inch circles, slightly thicker at the edges than in the center. Coat each pizza pan with ½ tablespoon melted butter and place dough in the pans. Brush dough with remaining butter. Top each pizza with half the sliced fruit and half the cherries. Sprinkle each with brown sugar.

2. Bake pizzas at 350°F for 20 minutes. Remove from oven and let stand for a few minutes. Serve warm.